Text by Tim Newark
Colour plates by Angus McBride
B/W illustrations by Edward Haney

Copyright © 2000
by CONCORD PUBLICATIONS CO.
603-609 Castle Peak Road
Kong Nam Industrial Building
10/F, B1, Tsuen Wan
New Territories, Hong Kong
www.concord-publications.com

We welcome authors who can help
expand our range of books. If you
would like to submit material,
please feel free to contact us.

We are always on the look-out for new,
unpublished photos for this series.
If you have photos or slides or
information you feel may be useful to
future volumes, please send them to us
for possible future publication.
Full photo credits will be given upon
publication.

ISBN 962-361-646-5
printed in Hong Kong

[dedication]
To Quentin, a secret master of ancient warfare

Project designed by Ken Mosbaugh
Inquiries regarding the sale of the paintings in this book
should be addressed to:
Paintings
4713 El Camino Avenue
Carmichael, CA 95608
U.S.A.
Fax: 916-973-8952

Ancient warfare covers three thousand years of conflict from the Sumerians and the Egyptians to the armies of Rome. It is one of the strangest periods in military history for many of its commanders embarked on war convinced that they were gods and their forces were invincible. Even the Romans, who embraced logic and science, were convinced of the divine nature of leadership. Augustus, first Roman emperor, believed that a heavenly radiance shone from his eyes and was displeased when anyone he glanced at failed to drop their head as though dazzled by the sun. The Celts believed that a dazzling light rose above the head of an heroic leader and the Romans were not averse to using this belief against the Celts when a centurion strode into battle with a glowing coal attached to his helmet. The Celtic tribesmen fled before him.

Alexander the Great was perhaps the most famous of these divine commanders, making a trek across the desert in Egypt to visit a shrine where he was greeted as the son of the god Ammon. Convinced of his own divinity, Alexander believed that success in battle really came down to the two opposing commanders and how their armies perceived them. If he could make the opposing commander run, then his army would collapse behind him. With this simple concept and wishing to waste no time with more complex tactics, Alexander defeated the Persian emperor twice, on both occasions charging directly at him and using the rest of his troops simply to hold the superior numbers of his enemy. When the Persian emperor rode off from the battlefield, fearing for his own life, despite an army of tens of thousands around him, Alexander was victorious. With this principal in mind, Alexander conquered one of the greatest empires in the ancient world.

The superhuman quality that ancient commanders believed they possessed is better understood today as charisma. It brought the best out of their warriors and convinced them to follow their leaders despite increasing hardships. The three greatest commanders of the ancient world—Alexander, Hannibal and Caesar—all had it. Caesar wore a scarlet cloak so that his soldiers could see him in the thick of battle and gain strength from it. Pharaohs and kings were all portrayed in the midst of battle on their public buildings as this was the greatest sign of ruling vigour. When a king was not present, an empire could rapidly collapse, like the fall of Babylon in 539 BC when the Persian warlord Cyrus simply walked into the city because its king had been absence and no longer commanded the faith of his people.

The importance of appearance in ancient warfare extended also to the nature of armies. The more extraordinary and impressive an army appeared, the more courage it took to stand before it. This reached a peak of spectacle in the Hellenistic era when the armies of rulers such as Antiochus the Great included numerous war elephants clad in armour, chariots protruding with spikes and scythes, phalanxes of men carrying spears over 20 feet long, and a variety of bizarre cavalry ranging from central Asian archers to heavily armed horsemen wrapped in armour from head to toe including face masks. Of course, it did not guarantee victory every time and one of the lessons of ancient warfare, so keenly appreciated by later generations, is how apparently battle winning elements such as war elephants could be defeated by simple tactics such as those employed by the Romans at Zama, allowing the elephants to pass harmlessly between columns of troops.

The history of ancient warfare is therefore an amazing journey through an exotic world, but a world that is subject to the laws of our own time. Exhausted unimaginative empires give way to more vigorous, single-minded powers.

Sumerian warband gather outside city temple in southern Iraq, c.2500 BC

(Plate 1)

Sumeria stands at the very beginning of military history. Two ancient Sumerian relics are the oldest evidence of organised warfare. The Standard of Ur in the British Museum in London, and the Stele of Vultures in the Louvre in Paris, show soldiers similarly clad in sheepskins or leather cloaks holding long spears and large rectangular shields, fighting together in a phalanx. These formations were preceded by skirmishers armed with slings and bows and were supported by solid chariots pulled by asses.

It is a way of war that would remain almost unchanged in its essentials—phalanx, skirmishers, cavalry—for four thousand years. It was the product of civilisation: agriculture produced a surplus that provided taxes that led to urban organisation that required defence from other competitive city states. On top of this, the Sumerians had mastered the production of bronze to create sharper, stronger weapons, and invented a form of writing and calculating time, all useful for the conduct of war.

Based in southern Iraq between the Tigris and Euphrates rivers, the Sumerian people lived in a series of city states, including Ur, Uruk, Umma, and Lagash. These were ruled by priest kings, who ran both the main temple and the city, combining religious and secular roles. They would also raise armies. The Sumerians themselves seem not to have been great conquerors, concerned mainly with battles amongst themselves. Eventually, the Akkadians, in the north of the region, took control of the area and subdued all the Sumerian cities. When the Sumerians reasserted themselves in the Third Dynasty of Ur, they approached war with a new realism and their triumph is partly credited to them employing Akkadian mercenaries, the more martial people. By the second millennium, the land of the Sumerians had become part of the Babylonian realm.

The painting shows two forms of chariot typical of the Sumerians. The four wheeled battle wagon is the earliest form of Sumerian chariot from the middle of the third millennium. Based on examples excavated from Sumerian cities, these wagons were narrow in construction with solid wooden sides and front backed with red-dyed ox-hide. The wheels were solid, being constructed out of three pieces of wood to enable a greater diameter than possible from the tree trunks available to them. Horses do not appear to have been available to pull the chariot, instead smaller animals such as asses were employed. With the driver in the front of the chariot, there was

room for only one warrior who appears to have been armed with javelins.

The so-called straddle car was a chariot derived from fixing wheels to an elongated draught-pole and placing a padded saddle over it. A quiver containing javelins and axes was fixed to the draught-pole. This was a lighter, faster vehicle than the battle wagon. In the background is an array of Sumerian warriors. They wear the sheepskin skirts and cloaks typical of this people who, after all, made their fortune out of grazing herds. They also wear leather cloaks and a variety of leather caps and copper helmets. They are armed with spears and axes, all tipped with bronze blades.

(Plate 2)

The early New Kingdom period in ancient Egypt saw a revolution in warfare. The incursion of middle eastern horse-culture tribes such as the Hyksos introduced the Egyptians to a more mobile form of warfare based on the chariot and the composite bow. Chariots provided quick moving bases for archers to move around the battlefield, a little like horse artillery in the modern era, thus being able to surround an enemy formation and break it with missile fire, before a final advance by foot soldiers wielding axes and spears. Having learnt from the Hyksos and thrown off their rule, the Egyptians of the New Kingdom embarked on an energetic series of campaigns. Nubia in the upper Nile was a natural area of conquest as it both secured their southern frontier and exerted control over trade with black Africa.

Although there is a new realism in the depiction of warfare in New Kingdom art, showing detailed representations of chariots and other paraphernalia of battle, the nature of combat seems to have changed little from earlier periods. Naked ambition is clothed in a religious garb of dispelling chaos and appeasing the gods with Pharaohs conducting wars as crusades in which defeated soldiers were executed as offerings to the gods. Abu Simbel reliefs show a scribe recording the number of severed hands taken from the enemy.

Expeditions to Nubia often took the form of grand raids in which the aim was not to grab land but terrorise the inhabitants into submission. An earlier Egyptian account describes one such raid: "Then I went upstream in victory, slaughtering the Nubian in his land, and came back downstream stripping crops, and cutting down the rest of their trees, so I could put fire to their homes, as is done against a rebel against the king." Such destruction could condemn a whole community to famine and death.

For the ordinary Egyptian soldier, the aim of warfare was personal opportunity. The acquisition of slaves and livestock was a primary objective, although soldiers frequently complained that the bulk of these would be handed over directly to their commanders. Foreign women were particularly prized, although these could cause trouble as one soldier recalls: "the foreign woman faints on the march; she hangs on to the soldier's neck. His knapsack drops, another grabs it while he is burdened with the woman." An extract from The Tale of Sinuhe gives a vivid description of hand-to-hand combat: "When he charged me, I shot him, my arrow sticking in his neck; he screamed; he fell on his nose; I slew him with his axe... Then I carried off his goods; I plundered his cattle. What he meant to do to me, I did to him. I took what was in his tent; I stripped his camp. Then I became great, wealthy in goods, rich in herd." The eternal dream of the soldier.

The painting shows the Pharaoh Horemhab in a chariot in combat with Nubian warriors. His chariot is typical of the light two-wheeled vehicles introduced into Egypt following Hkysos rule. This chariot is based upon an illustration on the tomb of Userhet as well as an example in the Museum of Florence. The structure is made of wood, including elm for the pole, pine for the tyres, birch for the cab, and was extremely light; illustrations survive of soldiers transporting chariots on their shoulders. The front of the cab was covered in leather stretched over the frame. The two horses pulling the chariot would not have been large animals, the remains of one uncovered at Thebes being no more than 12 hands high. The Pharaoh seems vulnerable in his robes to Nubian arrows and it may have been more likely, although there are no such depictions, that such an important warrior would have been clad in bronze scale armour, as examples of this have been found at Thebes.

The Egyptian soldiers in the painting are typical of the period, wearing the characteristic striped head cloth. They carry large animal skin shields which could be used in shield walls to protect against enemy arrows. They carry spears and the bronze sickle sword or khopesh, which was especially useful for decapitating prisoners. The Nubians wear animal skins and their hair is adorned with ostrich feathers. They shoot simple wooden bows, less powerful than Asiatic composite bows.

Muwattalis, King of the Hittites, late 14th century BC

(Plate 3)

The Hittites rose to power on the backs of the declining Mitanni in Syria in the 14th century BC. The Mitanni had suffered from the expansion of the Egyptians into Syria and although they made peace with them, the ruling dynasty was weakened by disputes between anti- and pro-Egyptian factions which led to assassinations and coups. The Hittites to the north-west of them in Asia Minor took advantage of this discord and expanded their own empire into this land, eventually dividing the Mitanni realm between themselves and the Assyrians from the east.

The Hittites were efficient rulers, binding vassal states with treaties and extracting tributes of gold and silver. Soldiers were required to swear loyalty to the Hittite army and proved their worthiness by marching between two posts, each having one half of a human sacrifice strapped to it. No evil could pass between these posts and thus the soldier was ritually cleansed. Soldiers were recruited from a wide area including the whole of Anatolia (Asia Minor) as far as the Aegean coast, as well as the former provinces of the Mitanni in Syria. The king was the supreme military commander and armies were organised in tens, hundreds and thousands. Other than the Egyptians or Mitanni, the main enemies of the Hittites were the Achaeans from the Greek islands and the Kaska, raiders from the highlands of northern Anatolia.

The Hittite way of warfare appears to have been influenced by their continuous guerrilla wars along the frontiers with their Anatolian enemies. Feigned retreats, night-time manoeuvres, the importance of gathering information and the use of this to spring ambushes were key elements of their success. In Syria, the Hittites adopted the methods of their neighbours, recruiting large numbers of chariots and favouring confrontational battles, where their massed chariots would charge an unprepared enemy. Large bodies of foot soldiers armed with spears were kept in reserve to either support or protect the chariots. The favourite chariot of the Hittites was a heavy vehicle with eight-spoked wheels on which could stand at least three men armed with bows or spears. Hittites charioteers aimed to close with their enemy's chariots, hoping that their heavier build and more numerous crew would overwhelm lighter chariots. Extra Hittite crewmen could also jump down from their chariots, allowing more flexible forms of assault.

Bronze scale and lamellar armour appears to have been invented in Syria around the 17th century BC and was employed by the Mitanni to great effect, giving them an initial battlefield advantage over their less well armoured adversaries. The Hittites adopted this form of armour in the form of long scale tunics and many chariot borne warriors armed with spears would be thus armoured. Their helmets surmounted by plumes were also adopted from the Mitanni. Hittite foot soldiers were mostly unarmoured wearing long sleeveless garments and carrying wickerwork shields covered in leather. They appear to have been largely clean-shaven, wearing their hair in long pigtails or scalp-locks, which allowed the Egyptians to disparagingly call them "women-warriors". The painting recreates these warriors.

When the Egyptian Pharaoh Ramesses II led his invading army towards Syria in 1301 BC, the Hittite vassal state of Amurru had little choice but to switch its allegiance to the Egyptian army at its gates. The news gave Muwattalis full warning that he must prepare to defend his Syrian realm or lose it completely to the aggressive Egyptians. Muwattalis sent out orders to his generals to gather a great army for the next year and planned to recover Amurru. It was one of the largest armies ever raised by the Hittites and included two massive formations of spearmen approximately 18,000 strong each, while some 2,500 chariots were to be employed in the first wave of attack with a reserve of another 1,000 chariots. With this formidable force, he would then confront the Egyptians in battle and annihilate them. The chosen area of combat was Qadesh.

Syrian archers, 14th century BC

(Plate 4)

The 18th dynasty was an expansive period for ancient Egypt. Having expelled the Hyksos, or "foreign rulers", a succession of Pharaohs went on the offensive and took Egyptian authority into the Near East with campaigns fought in Canaan (now Israel) and Syria. Aside from their chariots, an important aspect of the Egyptian way of warfare at this time was archery. Crowds of archers would be employed to bombard the enemy with arrows prior to any assault.

Generally expected to keep at a distance from the enemy, Egyptian archers wore little if any armour, although some more elite warriors may have been clad in scale armour. Archers could also be recruited from foreign troops and Syria had a long reputation for fine archery, borne out of the nomadic horse-archers who raided across its plains. This continued into the Roman era when Syrian archers were recruited to fight as far away as Scotland as part of the Imperial army.

The composite bow was the most powerful missile weapon in the ancient world. Its power derived from the combined strength of several materials sandwiched together. A wooden core was backed with layers of sinew and bellied on the inside with strips of horn. All these materials were then pressed together with an animal glue in a process which took much practice and was not easily mastered. The gluing of horn to wood was usually carried out in winter with cooler, humid conditions slowing and thus toughening the setting. Glue-soaked sinew was better applied on a warm spring day. The bow would be left to set for two months at least.

Campaigns were usually fought during the summer and autumn and when the fighting season was over, a composite bow would be unstrung and reconditioned. Adding strips of bone to the tips of the bow holding the string greatly improved its strength. The combination of wood, sinew and horn created a highly flexible bow which allowed a far longer draw than was usual from a similar sized wooden bow. It was thus ideal for use on horseback and was a favourite of all horse cultures in the Middle East, including Syrians, Persians, and Scythians. Longer composite bows were more accurate, but the strength needed to pull them required a firm foothold and so became the preserve of foot soldiers.

Recent experiments with bows have demonstrated the power of the composite bow against different forms of armour. Shooting at a range of 35 metres, several different shapes of socketed arrowheads managed to pierce a single layer of mail armour to a lethal depth. The doubling of mail, however, managed to prevent the penetration of arrows and this was practised by both Celts and Romans who wore two layers of mail over their shoulders. Scale armour proved much less predictable. Although all kinds of socketed arrows could penetrate it, they could also be stopped by it, depending solely on whether it hit the scales at the top and weaker point or whether it struck at the lower point where it overlapped other scales.

Arrows fired at plate armour failed to penetrate at all, even from a distance as close as seven metres. Arrows fired at the flanks of the armour just glanced off. Thus, the plate armour later worn by the Romans proved to be the most effective defence against Asian arrows. The wooden shield covered in leather also proved to be a most effective defence, no arrows penetrating this to a significant depth to harm the carrier. In the ancient Near East, when few warriors wore armour and most of this took the form of mail or scale armour, the Egyptian or Syrian archer was clearly king and explains the great use made of them by Egyptian warlords. As soon as warriors started using shields, however, and later plate armour, this archery became less decisive on the battlefield.

The painting shows three Syrian archers defending a fortified wall. They are unarmoured except for the wicker shield held by the middle archer. This archer also carries the triangular-shaped bow typical of ancient Egyptian armies. The archer in front has dipped his arrows into a pot of pitch to create flaming arrows to set alight the wooden siege engines of attackers. Flaming arrows were also created by attaching little linen bags containing inflammable material to arrow shafts and this being set alight. Syrian archers were in great demand as mercenaries from ancient Egypt to ancient Rome.

Egyptian Pharaoh Ramesses II at the battle of Qadesh in Syria, 1300 BC

(Plate 5)

In his late 20s and full of energetic ambition, Ramesses II knew the time had come for Egypt to challenge its great rivals in the middle east—the Hittites in Syria. Embracing the new form of chariot-borne warfare and with improved military organisation, the Egyptian army was a formidable war machine and Ramesses took it to its limits. In an exploratory campaign, he advanced along the Phoenician coast and attacked Amurru, a city loyal to the Hittites. With this gauntlet thrown down, both sides prepared for a major confrontation which took place the following year at the city of Qadesh.

Ramesses commanded an impressive force consisting of four armies or divisions named after gods—Amon, Re, Ptah and Sutekh—possibly numbering some 20,000 warriors. A considerable part of his army were foreign mercenaries, including Nubians, Sherdens (Sea-Peoples), Libyans and Canaanites. The Hittite king, Muwattalish, commanded an equally diverse army consisting of 18 vassal peoples amounting to some 3,700 chariots and 37,000 foot soldiers. Advancing in the spring of 1300 BC on a month long march into Hittite territory, Ramesses aimed for Qadesh, sited on the banks of the Orontes river, north of Beirut, dominating the strategic pass into the Bekaa Valley.

Bedouin deserters from the Hittite army gave Ramesses the news he hoped for—the Hittite king had lost his nerve and retreated rather than face the Egyptians at Qadesh. Ramesses now raced ahead with the Amon division to secure the city, leaving the rest of his army to catch up with him. The Hittite king, however, was far wiser than his adversary and it seems the Bedouins were not deserters at all, for Muwattalish was waiting near Qadesh with his entire army.

The next morning, after Ramesses had set up his camp outside the city, the Hittites chose to attack the other Egyptians marching quickly to catch up with their Pharaoh. The Re division was caught in open order and completely routed. They now ran towards the Amon camp and their panic undermined the morale of the warriors surrounding Ramesses. Faced with imminent disaster, Ramesses had to take personal command of his army and stood at the centre of the battle in his war chariot. Armed with a bow, Ramesses chose to stand and fight.

The heroic account of Ramesses stand is recorded in inscriptions

on the Great Temple at Abu Simbel. There, the relief shows the Egyptian camp surrounded by a stockade of large shields. Inside, there are details of ox-carts carrying food and supplies, a chariot being repaired, an archer re-stringing his bow and a soldier whose wounded leg is being tended. Ramesses great tent is surrounded by the smaller tents of his officers and he is shown talking to his generals while Hittite spies are beaten and interrogated. The paraphernalia of the Egyptian camp appears to have helped Ramesses, for the wave of triumphant Hittite chariots was broken by the mess of tents and in the confusion Egyptian and mercenary archers retaliated with a storm of arrows that further hindered the Hittites. Desperate hand-to-hand combat followed with axes and swords clashing with maces and spears.

When Hittites broke though into the royal enclosure, they faced the Pharaoh's Sherden bodyguard. Armed perhaps with round shields and horned helmets, the Sherdens demonstrated their worth by fighting hard and long, enabling Ramesses to organise a counter-attack in which his superior archery, borne by chariots, managed to turn the tide. With the approach of the rest of the Egyptian army, the Hittites decided they had had enough and retreated into the city. It was a bloody, drawn conflict, which could have ended in annihilation for Ramesses, if not for the loyalty of his mercenary troops. Ramesses now returned to Egypt, thanking the gods for his lucky escape, with his scribes already working on how to give an heroic spin to the whole affair.

The painting shows Ramesses II in his chariot awaiting the attack of the Hittites at Qadesh. His chariot shows how six spokes were now added to the wheels to give them greater strength to carry armoured archers and also compete with heavier Hittite chariots. The bowcase is decorated with the Pharaoh's lion motif. Ramesses is shown wearing the famous <u>khepresh</u>, or war crown, which was coloured blue and featured the sacred cobra on its brow. He wears a combination of gilded bronze scale armour and a corselet in the form of falcon wings.

Tiglath-Pileser III, king of Assyria, receives the acclamation of his warriors, late 8th century BC

(Plate 6)

Assyria was one of the great military powers of the ancient world. At its height, at the end of the second millennium and the beginning of the first millennium BC, it dominated the old Mesopotamian heartland, including Babylonia, and sent armies deep into Iran, Syria, Palestine and Turkey, as far as the Mediterranean coast. For several centuries, they lived off the rich tribute they extracted from intimidated city states. Numerous stone friezes survive in museums such as the British Museum in London, showing their aggressive, organised warfare. In the 9th century BC, Assyrian dominance wavered as internal rebellions and civil wars shook the realm. A military commander called Pulu saw his opportunity and took control of the situation—he assumed the royal name of Tiglath-Pileser III.

Tiglath-Pileser's strength was organisation. He reformed the government of the Assyrian empire by dividing the provinces into over eighty smaller administrative regions, each ruled by a governor, often a eunuch, who owed complete allegiance to the king. He introduced a communication system of riders bringing news from regional governors and spies in border regions. To punish rebels, he reintroduced the Assyrian policy of mass deportations, moving tens of thousands of people from one area to another. But at the heart of the Assyrian system was its army and Tiglath-Pileser thoroughly reformed it.

Previously, Assyrian soldiers were recruited from farm workers whose performance on campaign had to fit in with harvests. Tiglath-Pileser established a standing army of professional soldiers who could fight at any time. Warrior numbers were augmented by the use of mercenaries, including especially Aramaeans, but also, in later years, any conquered or available peoples, such as Greeks from Asia Minor and Scythians from central Asia. At the heart of the king's army was his Royal Guard or personal bodyguard. Further troops could be raised as regional levies, but the first two elements were always ready and formed the engine of the Assyrian war machine.

The Assyrian army was composed essentially of chariots, cavalry and infantry. Chariots had evolved from light two-horse vehicles into large four-horse, four-man vehicles, which served primarily as mobile bases for archers and also as a shock weapon which could be used in massed charges to break the enemy resolve. Cavalry was a major strength of the Assyrian army, consisting of armoured horsemen

fighting with bows and lances. These cavalry could operate in large independent raiding units a thousand strong and Tiglath-Pileser made sure that horses were at the top of his list of tribute goods. Conquests, however, were achieved by infantry. These consisted of archers, spearmen, slingers, and shield-bearers, many of them armoured. There were also specialist troops skilled at building and operating siege-machines for assaulting cities. With this new army, Tiglath-Pileser and his successors took the Assyrian empire to its greatest extent, including conquests in Persia, Asia Minor, Palestine, and Egypt.

The painting shows Tiglath-Pileser III in his command chariot surrounded by his loyal Assyrian troops. The chariot is an ornate example of the heavier four-man, four-horse chariots employed by the Assyrian army. It has heavier eight-spoked wheels. The huge parasol marks it as a command chariot and was either carried by a servant or attached to the vehicle. The warriors wear iron helmets and their spears are tipped with iron. The round shields are leather on a wicker base with a bronze boss.

Hoplites clash with Hoplites, Greece, 7th century BC

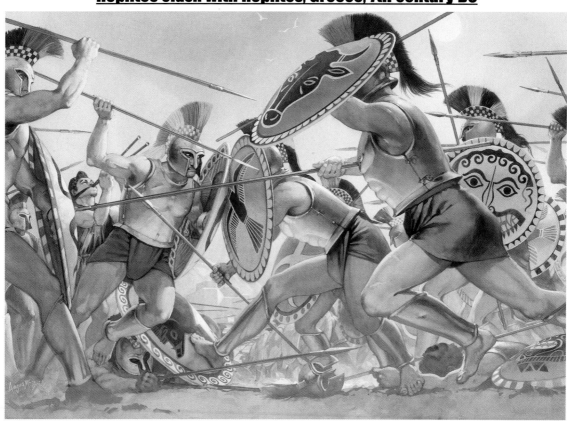

(Plate 7)

Hoplite battles in ancient Greece in the 7th century BC have been declared the birth of Western warfare. These were battles fought by citizen farmers who could not afford the time to embark on a long campaign. They were not professional raiders or bandits like the warriors of Asia who chose warfare as a way of life which continued year after year as they obtained loot through terrorising communities. These were responsible men who, if a conflict arose with a neighbouring state, wanted to resolve it in a day and the method they chose was to clad themselves in bronze armour and form dense packs of spear-carrying men, called phalanxes. These two formations would then clash with each other and the dispute would be decided by the end of the day. Then the warriors could go back to their farms. It was shock warfare and the tradition carries on today: confrontation rather than harassment is the Western way of war.

Initially, this hoplite way of fighting seems a brutal method of warfare. Two closely-packed groups of men running at each other with spears. The initial collision itself must have killed hundreds as the spears pierced any unguarded flesh. This was why, alone among warriors in the ancient world, the Greeks invented the heavy bronze breastplate—the name hoplite appears to be derived from the Greek word *hopla*, referring to this armour. The classic Greek breastplate was a quarter of an inch thick, made of bronze, and would quickly have become burning hot under the Greek sun. Bronze greaves were wrapped around the shin and bronze helmets, adorned with crests, protected the head. The early hoplites may have worn more armour, including thigh, arm and even foot armour. A large concave metre-wide shield, made of wood reinforced with bronze, was also carried, again unique to the Greeks in the ancient world.

The best fighters and most highly regarded citizens fought in the front row of the phalanx—it was an honour to do so and added to your social status. It makes good sense to have your best fighters in front, but if the clash of the phalanx was so devastating, then surely the first rank could be assured of a quick death. This contradiction gives a clue to the real nature of hoplite battles. It was a test of nerve, rather than a test of arms, and its basic nature was defensive. When the two phalanxes approached each other, men would naturally raise their shields to protect their groins and throats. They did not throw their spears, nor did they hold their spears in both hands to

plunge them deep into the opposing ranks (this would become the nature of phalanx warfare during Alexander's time when Greeks fought against foreigners).

Hopefully, the battle would be decided before either side even made contact. The first side to charge might so unnerve the others that they turn and run. Alternatively, if both sides were equally matched, then the two lines would make contact, seeking to protect themselves against spears used in a stabbing, probing way, and then push, thrusting their full body weight into their shields to batter the opponent backwards. Breastplates served to protect the warrior as much from the wildly thrusting weapons of his own side as the enemy in front. It was a deadly scrum and if you fell, you would be trampled by either side. Using spear then sword, the hoplites tried to establish their superiority in the crowd and then as one side felt itself pressed backwards, beginning to stumble, then that side would break. It appears hoplites did not pursue each other a long way as they had no wish to fight a war of extermination. It was enough to win and survive and then go back to their farms.

The painting opposite recreates the initial clash of hoplites. Those Greeks that could afford it would face their wooden shields with a veneer of bronze which would then be polished to shine in the sun and possibly temporarily blind their enemies. Most Greeks, however, simply painted their shields with terrifying images of either family or national significance.

Nabopolassar, king of Babylon, and the king of Scythia at the fall of Nineveh, 612 BC

(Plate 8)

For three centuries, the Assyrians dominated the ancient Middle East from Babylonia through Syria to Palestine. Their warriors were feared and their emperors grew rich, but even the Assyrian empire would have to face its decline and this came surprisingly quickly at the end of the 7th century BC. Scythian raiders from central Asia rode unhindered through the old Assyrian empire, ranging as far as Palestine in 633 BC. Egypt moved into the region of Palestine, filling the vacuum left by an increasingly ineffective Assyrian army. The sons of the great Assyrian king Ashurbanipal fought against each other and in Babylon a new ruler called Nabopolassar, "son of a nobody", seized power. This was one of Assyria's key cities, but the Assyrian army proved powerless to evict him. By 616 BC, Nabopolassar could see his enemy was a "paper tiger" and took the war to the Assyrians.

In 615 BC, the Medes, an Iranian people, took a chunk out of Assyria by capturing the cities of Arrapha and Ashur. Nabopolassar struck an alliance with the Medes and sealed this by having his son, Nebuchadnezzar, marry the daughter of the king of the Medes. Together, in 612 BC, they turned their attention to the mighty capital of the Assyrians, Nineveh. They were joined by the Scythians and three battles were fought outside the city before the massive walls were besieged. The Book of Nahum in the Old Testament describes the action. Siege machines were brought into place and great rams battered its walls. A river may have been diverted to undermine the walls as the palace topples down and Nineveh is described as "become like a pool of water".

The Hebrew Bible takes a delight in the end of this home of their Assyrian oppressors—"the lion's den"—and describes its agony in detail: "Spoil is taken, spoil of silver and gold; there is no end to the store, treasure beyond the costliest that man can desire. Plundered, pillaged, stripped bare! Courage melting and knees giving way, writhing limbs, and faces drained of colour... Ah! Blood-stained city, stepped in deceit, full of pillage, never empty of prey! Hark to the crack of the whip, the rattle of wheels and stamping of horses, bounding chariots, chargers rearing, swords gleaming, flash of spears! The dead are past counting, their bodies lie in heaps, corpses innumerable, men stumbling over corpses... Nineveh is laid waste; who shall console her?"

Such was the destruction of the city that it never rose again, becoming a mound of dust that just two hundred years later defied

identification. Assyria was finished and Babylonia was now the new power of the region. The painting opposite shows Nabopolassar, on the right, alongside the king of Scythia, centre. The Neo-Babylonians were heavily influenced by the Assyrians in their choice of clothing, weapons and armour. The Scythians, however, were from a completely different culture with its home in the steppes of central Asia. The Scythian warlord in scale armour is characteristically armed with bow and axe plus a sword. His weapons are gilded as befits his status.

The Scythians were the first great horse-culture people that we know of, being followed by the Huns and other Turkic warrior nations emerging from the same part of the world. Their primary weapon was the composite bow which they shot expertly from horseback. They preferred raiding tactics to confrontational battle. When forced to hand-to-hand combat, they fought with an axe or a curved sword. Herodotus describes how difficult they were to face in battle: "No one who invades their country can avoid destruction, and if they wish to avoid engaging with an enemy, that enemy cannot by any possibility come to grips with them. A people without fortified towns, living as the Scythians do, in wagons which they take with them wherever they go, used to fighting on horseback with bows and arrows, and dependent for their food not on agriculture but upon their cattle. How can such a people fail to defeat the attempt of an invader not only to subdue them, but even to make contact with them?"

Cyrus, king of the Persians, at the fall of Babylon, 539 BC

(Plate 9)

Out of the ashes of the Assyrian empire came an even stronger and bigger empire, that of the Persians. Like the Medes, they were an Iranian people, and it was the Medes who first appeared to be the stronger, playing a crucial role in bringing an end to the power of Assyria. Learning from the Medes, the Persians made their own bid for power around 550 BC. Cyrus, son of a king of Persia and the daughter of the king of the Medes, staged a mutiny within the army of the Medes and overthrew his grandfather. It was more a palace revolution than an act of conquest and the Persians merely took over what the Medes had already established, allowing the Medes to continue to enjoy their high position within the empire. It was simply under new and more vigorous management.

Cyrus the Great set about conquering lands beyond the frontiers of the Medes. He defeated the king of Lydia in Asia Minor to push his empire to the Aegean coast and in eastern Iran he took his army to the borders of India. Babylon was the key to the middle east and although Cyrus skirted around it for earlier conquests, there would come a time when he would have to face the Neo-Babylonians. That time came in 539 BC. Just thirty years earlier, the Babylonians had felt powerful enough to challenge the Pharaohs by attempting to invade Egypt. They failed, but Cyrus had enough respect for them to leave them alone as he took on easier opponents.

As the Persians consolidated their empire, word reached Cyrus of discontent within Babylon. Nabonidus, king of Babylon had left his capital for a ten year exile in Arabia, leaving his son as regent in charge of the capital. Perhaps fearing the intentions of Cyrus, Nabonindus returned to Babylon, but it was already too late. Cyrus led his army into the Babylonian realm in 539 BC and captured the city of Otis by assault. Nabonidus was fast losing support within his own capital and had to put down a revolt of his own people. The way was now clear for Cyrus. No one would fight against the Persian and he entered Babylon peacefully. Green fronds were placed before him as he entered the great city. Nabonidus was found lurking within the city walls and was put to death. Another palace coup had brought Cyrus the greatest jewel of the middle east.

The painting opposite shows Cyrus witnessing his victory in the temple at Babylon. There were two main dress styles within the Persian empire of Cyrus. One was the Persian which consisted of a long flowing patterned robe and can be seen worn by the elite imperial guardsmen recorded on the palace glazed bricks at Susa. The other is the Median style consisting of a long-sleeved tunic, trousers and cap with ear flaps. This is worn by the soldiers in the painting and is very much a central Asian style, demonstrating that the Medians were from northern Iran and were influenced strongly by the arms and tactics of the Scythian steppe culture. The soldier closest to Cyrus also wears scale armour, whereas the one in the background wears padded cloth and leather armour.

The Greek historian Herodotus describes further the principal armament of Persian warriors: "They wore soft caps called tiaras, multi-coloured sleeved tunics with iron scale armour looking like the scales of fish, and trousers. Instead of round shields (like the Greeks) they carry wicker shields with their bow-cases hanging beneath them. They carry short spears, large bows, cane arrows, and daggers hanging from their belts beside the right thigh." Visual evidence, however, disputes whether the Persians carried spear, bow, and shield all at the same time, although the frieze at Susa does show them carrying spears and bows, making the Persian infantry very flexible in both attack and defence. Other illustrations show Persian warriors fighting with axes and curved swords, just like the Scythians.

Battle of Salamis, 480 BC

(Plate 10)

The year 480 BC began as a disaster for the Greeks. Xerxes, emperor of the Persians had crossed the Hellespont and invaded mainland Greece. At the mountain pass of Thermopylae, an army of Greeks headed by Spartans confronted the Persians. Betrayed by a Greek who led the Persian army on a mountain path behind their position, the Greek army was surrounded and wiped out. Northern Greece was now wide open to the Persians, and Xerxes advanced southwards towards Athens. The majority of Athenians fled the city, except for a small garrison that turned the Acropolis into a fort. For two weeks, they held out against the Persians, but eventually they broke in and slew the defenders and ransacked the temple.

The Persian conquest seemed unstoppable and most Greeks wanted to draw a line of defence before the Peloponnese at the Isthmus, thus giving up the whole of central Greece, but Themistocles, commander of the Athenians, would not give up so easily. He wanted to challenge the Persians with a sea-battle at Salamis, but the rest were not interested. It was then he declared that if the other Greeks would not support him, then the Athenians would take their ships to southern Italy and leave Greece all together. The others reluctantly agreed and 378 Greek triremes gathered in the narrow waters near the island of Salamis at the entrance to the bay of Eleusis. Xerxes decided this concentration of Greek maritime force could not be left alone and directed his own larger fleet to attack it. Among the galleys of the Persian fleet were many belonging to Greeks from the Ionian coast of the Aegean, among them the female warlord Artemisia. She advised Xerxes not to attack, recommending he continue his land war, but the emperor was determined to snuff out this threat to his naval supply line.

Xerxes began the combat by sending troops ashore to the island of Salamis so that any Greeks swimming ashore from their ships would be slaughtered. The Greeks began to lose their nerve and considered abandoning the Athenians, but Themistocles sent a note to the Persian camp, pretending it was from a traitor, saying that the Greeks were going to sail away that night. Xerxes would not let this happen and closed the trap just as Themistocles hoped by blocking an escape route with his Egyptian fleet. The Greeks had no choice but to fight and in the morning they faced three main lines of Persian ships drawn up at the entrance to the sound. Xerxes had a huge throne made for him so he could watch the battle from a nearby hill.

The Phoenician allies of the Persians began the battle by moving in column towards the Greeks. The Athenians surged forward first, cutting off the Phoenicians from the rest of the Persian fleet, and drove them towards the shore.

The rest of the Persian fleet crowded into the narrow waters behind the Phoenicians and close fighting continued all day. The painting opposite recreates the kind of fighting at the height of the battle of Salamis with a Greek galley surging towards a Persian ship, hoplites on board launching their spears at the Persian warriors. Galleys rammed each other, splintering the sides of ships, some sinking under the impact, others becoming locked with each other. Armoured warriors clambered from one deck on to another, recreating land warfare at sea. Arrows flew from ship to ship while some were tipped with fire and set alight the wooden structures. In the chaos, Artemisia decided to break out, but she could only achieve this by sinking one of her own ships. Xerxes saw the action and misinterpreted it, recommending it to his officers, saying "My men have become women, my women men."

Artemisia's desperate action gives a clue to the nature of the fighting on that day. Confusion reined as Attic Greek fought against Ionian Greek and probably many ships were sunk by accident or mistake. It was this chaos that defeated the Persians with many ships of the Persian fleet being sunk by their own side. Xerxes had made a terrible mistake. He had handed the Greeks a victory and destroyed his own valuable fleet which served as a logistical support for his land army. It was a severe blow and Xerxes was forced to retreat from Greece, despite being undefeated on land. Strategically, it was a triumph for Themistocles.

(Plate 11)

The Etruscans were the early neighbours of the Romans, living in the area of central Italy now known as Tuscany. The Greeks called them Tyrrhenians and subsequent historians have never been quite sure if they were native Italians or Greek colonists. It appears most likely that the majority of the Etruscan population were Italian but their culture was influenced by Greek trader immigrants, just like in southern Italy. Their distinct civilisation is dated from around 700 BC until the 4th century BC when they were absorbed by Rome.

Militarily they were strongly influenced by the Greeks, their warriors fighting like hoplites with body armour, crested helmets and spears and shields. They fought against the Romans, placing Etruscan kings on the throne of Rome, and they fought for control of trade against Greeks in southern Italy and at sea, capturing Corsica in alliance with the Carthaginians. They expanded into northern Italy and established several towns, but this brought them into contact with the Celtic tribes advancing over the Alps and looking for their own settlements in the Po valley. In this tug of war, the Celts proved triumphant, forcing the Etruscans out of northern Italy in the 4th century BC. A burial stone inscription records a horseman from Etruscan Felsina fighting against a naked Celt. The painting recreates a Celtic raid against Etruscan warriors.

Etruscan relics gathered at the Villa Giulia and other museums in Rome give an insight into the character of Etruscan warfare. The famous "Mars of Todi", an Etruscan bronze statue of the late 5th century BC depicts an almost life-size warrior wearing a cuirass of scale or lammellar armour with reinforcing pieces running over his shoulders and secured to his chest. He wears an open-faced crested helmet with raised cheek-guards. His thighs are covered by a short skirt of strips of armour. The spear he is resting on is missing. Other pieces of armour on display include a pair of greaves, a bronze breastplate in two parts, a Celtic-style helmet, and part of a masked helmet.

It is thought that Etruscan armour began as cloth or leather with round or rectangular pieces of metal attached to it and then developed into completely bronze breastplates. Greek-style helmets are common, but a distinctly Etruscan-style bronze helmet was found in Greece where it had been given as an offering to the gods at Olympus following the Greek victory over the Etruscans at Cuma in 474 BC. This is now located in the British Museum in London. The hemispherical helmet looks like a cooking pot with a strengthening ridge down the centre of it. There is evidence of attachments for cheek-guards, a neck guard, and a crest or plumes. Shields were either round or elliptical with a wooden frame covered in leather or bronze.

Etruscan weapons included the spear with metal butt, the javelin, a triangular short sword, a sickle-like sword, a curved sacrificial knife, a double-headed axe, iron and bronze arrow-heads though no bows have been found, and the sling made of leather used to launch stones or lead acorn-shaped missiles.

(Plate 12)

Having beaten the Persian Emperor Darius at Issus and forced him to flee eastwards, Alexander marched southwards to conquer Syria and the Phoenician coast. This edge of the Mediterranean was vital for two reasons: first, its ports maintained the Persian fleet and their capture would weaken the Emperor's sea power; second, the trading cities were immensely rich and would increase substantially the wealth of Alexander and his warriors.

Tyre was one of these rich Phoenician ports, but unlike its neighbours, who sent their ambassadors to pay homage to Alexander, Tyre would not submit to the Macedonian. He was refused permission to make a sacrifice at their temple of Hercules. The Tyrians felt confident in the strength of their city, with it high walls, sited on an island rock and protected by 80 ships. Alexander, however, was determined to take it. He saw it as the most important naval base on the coast and could not conquer Egypt with it still in Persian hands. But how to capture it? It was separated from the mainland by more than half a mile of sea-water. Without a major fleet to support him, there was only one way Alexander could achieve its conquest. He would have to build a causeway, or mole, across the water.

At first, it was relatively easy to build the causeway as the water was shallow near the coast, but as it approached the island, the water became much deeper. At the same time, Tyrian galleys rowed out of its harbours and attacked the Macedonians. Alexander erected two great towers on the causeway and mounted siege artillery on them that could fire bolts and rocks at the attacking ships. Protective screens of leather were hung over the labourers building the causeway. But the Tyrians replied by sending fire ships floating towards the towers, sending them up in flames.

Alexander's will remained undeterred. He widened the causeway to take more towers and siege artillery, and then he got the break he needed. Two Phoenician fleets heard that their cities had submitted to Alexander and they sailed to Tyre to place themselves at his service. The Macedonians now outnumbered the ships of Tyre and the battle swung in his favour. The Tyrian fleet would not fight them and chose instead to block the mouths of the two island harbours. Alexander shifted his attention back to the causeway and began to use siege engines to batter the massive 150 foot walls. Siege engines were even placed on ships and boulders preventing their close access to the walls were hauled out. Tyrian

divers swam out and cut the cables of these boats, but Alexander replaced them with chains and cleared the way so his siege ships could batter at the walls.

The Tyrians made one last assault on the besieging fleets and drove one of them to the shore, but Alexander cut them off with his other ships and disabled them. Still the main walls opposite the causeway would not be breached, but Alexander's men concentrated on a weaker point near the southern harbour and eventually they broke it down. Alexander now planned a massive attack against this weak point and with his warriors in boats, they stormed the walls. Simultaneous attacks elsewhere on the island distracted the defenders and Alexander's men extended their control of the city. The defenders paid a heavy price for their defiance, 8,000 of them being slaughtered and the rest sold into slavery. It was a signal to every other city that confronted Alexander—surrender or be destroyed.

In the painting opposite, Alexander is shown supervising an attack on Tyre from the causeway. A siege tower is in flames, but bolt-throwing artillery is being rolled forward. Alexander is portrayed wearing a helmet similar to that on the Sidonian sarcophagus made for a ruler of the city of Sidon that surrendered without a struggle the previous year. It bears the curled horned imagery that Alexander favoured for his official representations, associating himself with the god Dionysus.

Alexander the Great's army defeats Indian warriors at the battle of Hydaspes in northern India 326 BC

(Plate 13)

For Alexander the Great, the conquest of Asia had a very clear point. He was a god and he was replicating the adventures of another—Dionysus, the god of wine and sensuality—who led his drunken hordes to the Far East. This was no political campaign, no intellectual or strategic endeavour to create a new world order—it was, for want of a more contemporary metaphor, a rock 'n' roll tour, where loot, ego satisfaction and personal pleasure were the important factors.

Every so often, Alexander and his troops found actual evidence that proved they followed in the path of Dionysus. On the northern border of India near Jelalabad, they came across a town called Nysa. Mount Nysa was the mythical home of Dionysus where he was born from the thigh of Zeus and nursed by nymphs. Nearby was a hill whose named resembled the Greek word for thigh and whose slopes were covered in ivy, the plant most associated with the god. With such supernatural reassurances, Alexander persuaded his men onwards through the Khyber Pass into India. They defeated several local tribes and crossed the great river Indus. Moving further south, he collided with the only native power that could equal his military strength. At the river Hydaspes, Porus confronted him with an army some 30,000 strong. Heavy tropical rain slowed Alexander's progress and although he brought many boats with him to cross the river, Porus and his warriors and his great war elephants stood directly across the water. Alexander was particularly concerned about the elephants, knowing they terrified the horses of his cavalry.

Alexander decided to use psychology in his battle with Porus. He gathered large stores of food indicating that he was staying for some time on the opposite side of the river. He then assembled his troops and marched them along the riverbank, giving Porus the impression he was about to attack. The Indians shadowed him, but it was purely a bluff. The sound of trumpets and marching warriors wearied Porus, who believed that Alexander was losing his nerve and stopped shadowing the invaders up and down the river. Alexander now seized upon a little island in the middle of the river covered in foliage and his troops quietly gathered to cross the river under the cover of the island. Alexander's army at this time was an exotic assembly of troops. They included his most faithful Macedonian warriors—hypaspists, two regiments of the phalanx, and two battalions of his elite Companion cavalry—Indian and Scythian horsemen, including mounted archers, and Agrianians armed with javelins.

Wind and rain helped to further conceal the crossing of the Hydaspes and Alexander finally managed to assemble his army on the other side of the river. His soldiers numbered only half of the Indian force opposing them, but Alexander, as always, made up for his inferiority in numbers with aggressive command and led his cavalry towards the camp of Porus. His gamble paid off and he scattered an advance guard of war chariots and horsemen. Porus, however, was alerted and his mighty army quickly assembled, with some 200 war elephants in the front-line. Alexander hoped to avoid these terrifying beasts and used his cavalry to provoke the Indian cavalry and thus break apart the opposition. His horse-archers and Companions succeeded in part, but the war elephants advanced and trampled the Macedonian foot soldiers.

Alexander kept a tight control of his cavalry and attacked again and again. The war elephants found themselves in the middle of a crush of warriors. Arrian, the main ancient source for this battle, describes the fate of the beasts: "Many of the animals had been wounded, while others, riderless and bewildered, ceased altogether to play their expected part and, maddened by pain and fear, set indiscriminately upon friend and foe, thrusting, trampling, and spreading death before them."

Alexander now had his foot soldiers advance in close-order with shields and spears protecting them from the elephants and, with himself leading the cavalry, he rallied his men to attack relentlessly. Eventually, his aggression paid off and the Indian army began to disintegrate. Porus, however, remained fighting, from the seat of his war elephant until wounded. Alexander sent a rider after the Indian warlord and asked him how he wished to be treated. "Like a King," said Porus. Alexander agreed and allowed him to keep his territory so long as he remained loyal to Alexander.

The painting shows Alexander's elite foot soldiers, or Foot Companions, mostly native Macedonians who wore armour and carried shields, fighting with swords and spears. One of their shields is painted with the head of a god, possibly an interpretation of Dionysus, the god whom Alexander emulated in his conquest of the east. Officers wore feathers on their bronze Phrygian helmets. Indian warriors are shown dead and defeated in a war chariot and around an elephant.

28

Carthaginian and Celtic warriors, 218 BC

(Plate 14)

Rome's worst nightmare—a Carthaginian and a Celtic warrior side by side—the wealth of Carthage combined with the legendary ferocity of the Celts. The Romans had already learned the hard way that fighting the Celts of northern Italy could be a lethal activity. Roman chronicler Livy describes the impact of a Celtic charge on Roman warriors: "The Celts, standing up and holding their weapons on board their chariots and wagons, bore down on them with a terrible noise of horses' hooves and wheels and panicked the Romans' horses with their strange din. Thus the (Roman) cavalry were scattered in this frenzy, their blind fear overthrowing them, both horses and riders. Their confusion spread to the standards of the legions and many of the first line were trampled underfoot by the horses and vehicles sweeping through the army. As soon as the Celtic foot soldiers saw their enemies in disorder they came at them, not leaving them a moment to regain their breath."

In 218 BC, the nightmare became a reality when war was declared between Carthage and Rome. Carthage was an immensely rich trading centre based in that part of the African Mediterranean now known as Tunisia. Its dominion ran along the entire north African coast into Spain. Its wealth arose from all forms of trade but especially dealing in precious materials such as African ivory and gold and even Cornish tin. They had already defeated Greek traders in this part of the Mediterranean and earlier in the 3rd century fought a war with Rome over control of Sicily. After many years of fighting, the Romans eventually won this struggle but when they invaded Africa they were soundly defeated by the Carthaginians outside their capital.

Later in the 3rd century, the Celts launched a massive assault on central Italy and the Romans retaliated by conquering northern Italy. If only the Carthaginians had timed their war with that of the Celts, then the Romans might have been crushed between two mighty powers. Such a thought occurred to Hannibal, commander of the Carthaginian army from 221 BC. With little chance of defeating the Romans at sea, Hannibal now considered a land invasion through northern Italy, in which the Carthaginians could rely on the hatred of the native Celts for their Roman conquerors. He would bring this nightmare to the land of the Romans.

In 218 BC, the Second Punic War broke out. Hannibal secured his control of Spain and established contacts with the Celtic chieftains of the Alps and northern Italy. They pledged their support to him, allowing him to pass through their territory and providing him with their finest Celtic warriors. Hannibal was used to dealing with foreign soldiers—the majority of the Carthaginian army was made up of mercenaries, most of them north Africans, including Numidian cavalry, as well as a large portion of Spanish and Celt-Iberian warriors. The strength of Hannibal's army in Spain was impressive, said to number 90,000 infantry, 12,000 cavalry and 40 elephants. Assured of a friendly Celtic welcome in northern Italy, Hannibal then took his army along the coast of southern France and over the Alps. The Roman nightmare was coming true and there was little they could do about it. A first clash at Ticinus demonstrated Hannibal's superiority as he swept aside the Romans. A more substantial Roman force braced itself for a confrontation at Trebia. Just before the battle, some Celts in Roman employment decided to leave and join the Carthaginians. They took with them a little present for Hannibal—some Roman heads.

Little is known about the appearance of Carthaginian warriors, but the reconstruction opposite shows a soldier of general Hellenistic style with a tunic of mail similar to that worn by his Roman opponents. The sword he carries is a falcata, an elegant curved weapon typical of the Spanish in this period. Although the majority of the Carthaginian army were mercenaries, there was a core of Libyan-Phoenician warriors, recruited from the original trading settlers of Carthage, and this warrior may have been one of them. The Celtic warrior is clad in the rich array of a chieftain, including iron helmet and mail shirt.

30

(Plate 15)

The Romans thought they had the Carthaginians beaten. Their second war would be a simple affair. A small army would hold Hannibal in Spain while their superior fleet would assault Carthage. But by the time they were assembling this strategy, Hannibal was already crossing the Alps and entering Italy. He arrived with a force much smaller than that which he could raise in Spain, little more than 26,000 men, but within two months he was conquering northern Italy. The Roman commander, Scipio Africanus, retreated before him, the local Celtic tribesmen keenly throwing in their lot with the Carthaginians. Joined by Sempronius Longus, now recalled from his intended invasion of Africa, the combined Roman forces determined to make a stand at the river Trebia, a tributary of the Po.

Hannibal liked to prepare his battles thoroughly and studied the landscape around the Trebia where the Romans were camped. On the edge of the Apennine mountains, the land was cut by several streams in deep gullies. They were good places to hide troops and during the night before the battle, Hannibal sent out 1,000 foot soldiers and 1,000 horsemen to hide along the stream beds running down from the hills. In the morning, he ordered his Numidian cavalry to ride forward and provoke the Romans in their camp to attack. The Romans were under the command of Sempronius and when he saw the Numidians galloping forward he ordered his own cavalry to ride out and meet them, to be followed by the rest of his army. The Numidians then retreated as ordered, drawing on the entire Roman army.

It was a bleak wintry day and snow flew in the face of the Romans but they were determined to catch the Numidians and punish Hannibal. They followed the African cavalry across the Trebia river, stumbling through the icy shallow water up to the other side towards Hannibal's camp set against the hills. Hannibal drew up his troops in front of his camp and the two armies clashed head on, Roman legionaries battling hard with the Spanish, Celts and Africans in the centre of Hannibal's army. The Numidians surged around the flanks of the Romans. As the battle raged, it was then that the Carthaginians hidden in the stream beds rose out of their positions and surprised the Romans in the rear, completely encircling them. Panic undercut the resolve of the Romans and their army began to dissolve, intent less on winning than surviving, cutting their way out across the Trebia.

Roman chronicler Livy describes the desperate fighting at the end of the battle: "a body of some 10,000 Romans—now completely surrounded—took the only way of escape they could find and hacked a passage with the edge of the sword right through the African centre and its Celtic allies... those who made for the river were either drowned or cut down as they hesitated on the brink... a few, emboldened by sheer terror of death by the sword, plunged into the water, got across and reached their camp."

The painting opposite shows the point when Numidian cavalry chased the Romans into the Trebia. The Numidians were supreme light cavalry. They were recruited from the tribes of the north African hinterland, corresponding to the area now known as Algeria. Their horses had neither bridles, bits nor stirrups, and the Africans rode bareback, controlling their mounts with their legs. They wore little armour, carrying usually a light shield and fighting with javelins.

Hannibal used them as mounted skirmishers, probing and provoking the enemy to do what he wanted them to do, at which point the Numidians would retreat and hide behind the other more substantial parts of his army, only to be unleashed again when the enemy were beaten and they could pursue the fleeing soldiers. Hannibal's elephants are shown in the background. The Romans wear either mail armour or little breastplates (the *pectorale*) typical of the Republican army at this time, plus Greek-style helmets.

Carthaginian war elephant attacking Romans, 218 BC

(Plate 16)

Hannibal is most famous for his use of war elephants. Used by other Hellenistic armies throughout the Mediterranean, the elephant was an impressive but temperamental addition to any army. Hannibal obtained his elephants in Morocco on the edge of the Sahara desert. They were used in the first Punic war against the Romans to tremendous effect, shattering Roman morale and breaking their armies, until the Romans captured several of the animals and became a little more used to them. When Hannibal planned to invade Italy, he considered it essential to bring several war elephants with him. It was no easy task.

Crossing the river Rhone on the way to Italy was just one of many major obstacles faced by Hannibal and his elephants. A jetty was constructed of several rafts strung together which were then covered with earth to make them look like an extension of the riverbank. Using female elephants to tempt the male war elephants on to end of the jetty, soldiers then cut loose the rafts and they floated across the river. Some elephants panicked, however, and fell into the river, using their trunks as snorkels and wading across under the water. The Alps, however, were the ultimate test. Livy describes the terrible impact they had on the Carthaginians: "towering peaks, snow-clad pinnacles soaring to the sky, rough huts clinging to the rocks, beasts and cattle shrivelled with cold, people with wild and ragged hair, all nature stiff with frost."

As they embarked on their 15-day trek across the mountains, the Carthaginians were ambushed by local tribesmen who threw down rocks on the passing soldiers. The elephants panicked on the tight mountain paths, but their handlers worked hard to calm them, eventually discovering they were the best weapons they possessed as the local tribesman had never before seen such huge beasts and ran away from them. Thus, the elephants could clear the mountain paths of both enemy warriors and real debris flung down in their way.

Other than the spectacle of crossing the Alps with elephants, the greatest use of war elephants in the ancient world was by Seleucis, one of Alexander the Great's generals, who shared with him the experience of fighting against the Indian army of King Porus at Hydaspes. Seleucis was so impressed by this that he considered them a battle-winning element and later when he ruled his own empire, he employed great numbers of them in his army. At the battle of Ipsus in 301 BC, he defeated his rival Antigonus with 480 war elephants.

The elephants employed by Macedonian warlords were Indian beasts, whereas though used by the Carthaginians were African. Elephants eat vast amounts of grass and leaves and it has been estimated that the 500 animals of Seleucis would consume some 110 tons of food a day. Elephant handlers would deal with this constant demand by chaining them by the legs at night and allowing them to forage in the countryside.

Despite their battle-winning reputation, elephants could also be a liability in combat. At the battle of Thapsus, Caesar noted what happened when archers and slingers hurled their missiles at a mass of elephants: "terrified by the whistling of the sling-shot and the showering stones and lead bullets, (the elephants) turned round and began to trample down their own side's soldiers, who were densely formed behind them." Caesar also recorded the bravery of a Roman legionary in attacking an elephant who had trampled an unarmed camp follower: "When the elephant saw the soldier coming at it with his javelin at the ready, it abandoned the corpse and wrapped its trunk around the soldier, lifting him up in the air. The soldier hacked at the trunk with his sword until the pain forced the elephant to drop the soldier. Trumpeting loudly, it turned round and ran back to join the other beasts."

In the painting opposite, the Carthaginian war elephant is supported by an array of soldiers, including Celts, Celt-Iberians, Spanish, Africans and Carthaginians.

Carthaginians attack Romans at the battle of Zama, 202 BC

(Plate 17)

Despite invading Italy and crushing the Roman army at several battles, Hannibal failed to conquer Roman Italy. Without the support of reinforcements, there was little Hannibal could achieve. In the meantime, the Roman fleet maintained its ascendancy and the war swung against Carthage. Scipio Africanus gained the confidence of the Roman Senate to launch an attack on Africa. Once there, he desperately sought to break away the Numidians from their alliance with Carthage and succeeded in winning the support of Masinissa.

Hannibal was now recalled from Italy and although the Carthaginians were in the process of negotiating a peace treaty with the Romans, Hannibal was determined to fight one last great battle against the Romans and save his people from defeat. That battle was fought at Zama in 202 BC and Livy described it grandly: "the two most famous generals and the two mightiest armies of the two wealthiest nations in the world advanced to battle, doomed either to crown or destroy the many triumphs each had won in the past."

Both sides numbered about 40,000 troops. Hannibal had gathered a large elephant corps, but was weakened by the lack of Numidian cavalry. Scipio's forces, in contrast, were battle hardened and his cavalry reinforced by the Numidians of Masinissa. Hannibal began the battle with a mass charge of elephants, but the Romans in Scipio's army were no longer the easily panicked troops of Italy who fled before elephants. They had been trained in special tactics to deal with this and their units opened wide columns in their formations, allowing the elephants to pass harmlessly between them. The painting opposite recreates this moment with mail-clad Roman warriors hurling their javelins at the elephants.

Scipio now took the offensive and tried to outflank the Carthaginians, but Hannibal had anticipated this and as his two front lines of troops moved to cover the threat, his third line of Italian veterans acted as a reserve to hold the centre. After much inconclusive fighting, both sides decided on a straight forward frontal attack and it came down to sheer hard fighting and stamina. Some Carthaginian mercenaries in the front line, including Celts and Moors, began to lose their nerve and tried to withdraw through the ranks behind them, but their comrades would not have it. "(The mercenaries) suddenly turned and fled to mingle with their own men," recorded Livy, "some finding refuge in the second line, others cutting down their comrades who refused to let them through, crying that they had not been given support before and were now refused a place in their ranks. By this time there was almost two battles in one as the Carthaginians were forced to fight both the enemy and their own men."

A combination of Roman and Numidian horsemen eventually triumphed over the Carthaginian cavalry and drove them off their field, but rather than pursuing them they showed good discipline and returned to attack the rear of the Carthaginian army. Hannibal was now encircled, just as he had surrounded the Romans in Italy, and his army was slaughtered. With Hannibal's power so soundly broken, a peace was hastily agreed and the Second Punic War was over with Rome triumphant throughout the Mediterranean.

Seleucid war elephant, 190 BC

(Plate 18)

Hellenistic is the term used to refer to the Greek-influenced kingdoms left behind after Alexander the Great's empire rapidly crumbled after his death. His warlord successors carved up his conquests and established themselves in various kingdoms across Asia. The Seleucid dynasty, founded by Seleucis I, ruled in Babylonia from 312 BC and in Syria from 301 to 64 BC. By the beginning of the 2nd century BC, the Seleucid king Antiochus III was re-establishing Seleucid rule over much of neighbouring Asia. He had subdued Persia and Bactria to the borders of India and he dominated Syria and Palestine. He then moved into Asia Minor where he laid claim to Greek cities along its Aegean coast. Greeks were beginning to view him as a new Alexander and he acquired the title "the Great".

The conquests of Antiochus brought him to the attention of Rome, the other great power in the Mediterranean, and rulers who had much to fear from the Seleucids, now turned to the Romans for help, like Eumenes II of Pergamum, a little kingdom in Asia Minor. The Roman general Flamininius warned Antiochus to leave alone the independent Greek cities of Asia Minor. But Antiochus proved he had a stronger legal claim to them and the fact that the Roman general then evacuated his troops from Greece, gave the Seleucids no cause for concern. It was then that Hannibal, arch-enemy of the Romans, appeared on the scene. Having evaded the Romans, he made his way to the court of Antiochus. For the Romans this really was a cause for concern. Rumours now circulated that Hannibal would invade Italy with a Seleucid army to help him.

Antiochus stepped back from the brink and coolly received Hannibal, preferring to engage in peace negotiations with the Romans, but in 192, temptation got the best of him and at the invitation of the Aetolians, he invaded Greece. Rome replied with a declaration of war and army of 20,000 troops under the command of consul Glabrio. Antiochus retreated before the Romans until he reached the famous pass of Thermopylae, where the ancient Persians 300 hundred years earlier had crushed the Spartans in a desperate last stand. Aware of his history, Glabrio sent his troops along the mountain pass that had helped the Persians defeat the Spartans, and attacked the Seleucid flank. Antiochus had chosen Aetolians to protect his flank but they proved weak allies and fled before the Romans. Antiochus now had to flee too and lost his entire army.

Antiochus was on the defensive and the Romans pursued him with their usual thoroughness. Joined by the Pergamese, but still outnumbered by the army of Antiochus over two to one, the Romans invaded Asia Minor and caught the Seleucid king in battle at Magnesia in 190 BC. Antiochus used his cavalry in a dashing attack that broke the Roman left wing, but the Roman centre stood its ground and the Seleucid cavalry left the battlefield in their pursuit. The Romans now counter-attacked, shattered the Seleucid left wing and so panicked the magnificent war elephants of Antiochus that they stampeded into the solid formation of his phalanx at the centre of his army. The Romans broke into the phalanx and the Seleucid army dissolved. Antiochus was beaten and had to agree to peace terms that favoured Rome.

The painting opposite depicts one of Antiochus' famous war elephants. It is an African elephant and its ears have been painted red to make it even more fierce. The scale armour worn by the elephant is based on a statuette, while the crest is inspired by that worn by horses into battle. The tower was secured on the back of the elephant by three giant straps around the chest, belly and under the tail. The warriors wear armour of Macedonian influence, reflecting the source of Seleucid power in the earlier conquests of Alexander.

(Plate 19)

Julius Caesar knew the strengths and weaknesses of the Celtic Gauls better than any other Roman and he used this knowledge to systematically conquer Gaul within eight years. He believed they were a once mighty people that had grown soft. "There was a time when the Gauls were more warlike than the Germans," he wrote, "when they actually invaded German territory." But now, living near a Roman province and receiving luxury goods by ship, they no longer had the hunger that made them conquer other people. "Gradually accustomed to inferiority and defeated in many battles, they do not even pretend to compete with the Germans in courage." They needed other people to protect them and one such person was Caesar with his Roman legionaries. When they called for help against the Germans, Caesar happily obliged and began to take apart Celtic Gaul in the process.

Part of Caesar's success was his thorough knowledge of the enemy he fought. His chronicles of the conquest of Gaul are part geography in which he makes notes on the customs and culture of the Gauls. One interesting observation is their feudal approach to battle. He describes two major classes of Gauls, the Druids and the Knights. When a campaign is to be fought, these Knights take to the field "surrounded by their servants and retainers, of whom each knight has a greater or smaller number according to his birth and fortune. The possession of such a following is the only criterion of position and power that they recognise." That great men were surrounded by their retainers and servants in battle gives a model for medieval warfare for 1500 years afterwards. Here, we do not have a Roman approach to war in which different troop types fought in different groups, but in which different troop types were mixed together in battle groups according to their loyalty to their feudal master. This was how most medieval battles were fought and shows an unbroken continuity between ancient Gaul and medieval France.

The final confrontation between the Gauls and Caesar was enacted in 52 BC when Vercingetorix led a rebellion against the Romans. Vercingetorix was a powerful personality who compelled his Celtic neighbours to submit to him. Caesar plunged into central Gaul after him, but was shaken by the Gauls at Gergovia. His own troops were surprised by the arrival of friendly Gauls who failed to leave their "right shoulders uncovered in an agreed sign". Caesar now recruited German cavalry, but the Gauls were encouraged by this

success and more and more of them rallied to Vercingetorix. At the great hill fort of Alesia, Vercingetorix hoped to crush Caesar between the walls of his stronghold and arriving Celtic reinforcements, but Caesar applied Roman methodical persistence and built a double wall of earthworks that protected his Romans both from the defenders and any arriving second army.

When the Gallic force arrived, Caesar fought one of the hardest battles of his life. "Some of the Gauls flung javelins," he recalled, "while others advanced to the attack with shields locked together above their heads, fresh troops continually relieving them when they were tired. All of them threw earth on to the fortifications, which enabled them to climb the ramparts and covered the obstacles hidden in the ground." Caesar, wearing a red cloak, was compelled to lead the defence and by bringing in reserve troops, the Gauls were eventually forced to flee, leaving Vercingetorix still locked in his fort. Alesia faced starvation and Vercingetorix had to surrender. The independence of the Gauls was over.

The painting opposite shows a Celtic assault on a Roman shield wall. The Romans hoped to halt the impetus of the charge with their weighted javelins. The bare-chested warrior wears tartan trousers, a typically Celtic pattern remarked upon by ancient authors. Gilded torques, a sign of personal freedom, are worn around the neck.

(Plate 20)

When Caesar invaded Britain in 54 BC, he was confronted by a very distinct form of fighting by the Celts who lived there. "In chariot fighting," he wrote, "the Britons begin by driving all over the field hurling javelins, and generally the terror inspired by the horses and the noise of the wheels are sufficient to throw their opponents' ranks into disorder." The chariots then halt and the warriors jump down from the platforms to fight on foot. In the meantime, the charioteers retreat a short distance, only returning when it looks as though their masters might need assistance for a quick exit.

"Thus they combine the mobility of cavalry," Caesar observed, "with the staying-power of infantry. By daily training and practice, they attain such proficiency that even on a steep incline they are able to control the horses at full gallop, and to check and turn them in a moment. They can run along the chariot pole, stand on the yoke, and get back into the chariot quick as lightning."

Later, Caesar describes an encounter where the Celts swooped out of cover and attacked the Romans in front of their camp. Roman legionaries were apparently too heavily armoured to pursue the fast-moving Britons. Even his cavalry found it difficult to deal with the chariots. "The Britons would generally give ground on purpose," he recalled, "and after drawing them some distance from the legions would jump down from their chariots and fight on foot, with the odds in their favour." Over a hundred years later, during the campaign of Agricola against the Britons, Tacitus records that the Britons were still using chariots, "noisily manoeuvring" between the British ranks.

Although Celtic chariot burials are found throughout Europe, it seems peculiar to Britain that they were retained long after they disappeared in warfare elsewhere. Accounts of ancient Irish warfare are also dominated by chariots. The British two-wheeled chariot evolved from heavier, four-wheeled carts found in tombs before the 5th century BC. Their spoked wooden wheels were bound with iron tyres and the hubs were wrapped with iron bands, while the wheels were held on the axle by iron linch-pins. Two horses pulled the chariot, linked by a yoke to a wooden pole, and were frequently clad in decorated metal and enamel harnesses or sometimes bronze masks. There is no archaeological evidence of scythes attached to chariot wheels, but the ancient Irish epic poem *The Tain* does refer to a chariot covered with "iron sickles, thin blades, hooks and hard spikes. Its stinging nails fastened to the poles and thongs

and bows and lines of the chariot, lacerating heads and bones and bodies."

The painting opposite shows the pre-battle display of Celtic British charioteers, darting back and forth in front of the assembled Roman ranks. Caesar had little difficulty in defeating the principal Celtic chieftain of southern England, Cassivellaunus, in battle, and capturing his stronghold, but he was bothered by the relentless guerrilla tactics of the Britons. He recalled his legionaries were "unnerved by the unfamiliar tactics and the enemy daringly broke among and got away unhurt." In one such encounter, one of Caesar's tribunes was killed. The Romans were reluctant to pursue them and leave their precious standard-bearers behind.

Ancient Helmets and Headgear

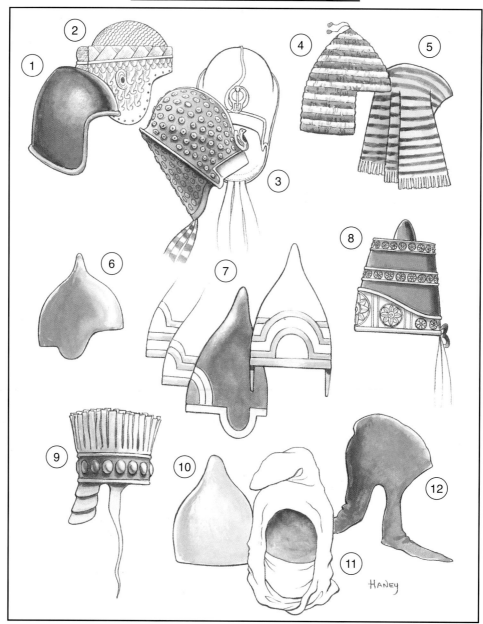

HANEY

Helmets as armour were not the first concern of many ancient warriors. Many were made of soft materials that could hardly ward off a strong blow and were mainly decorative, either intended to associate the warrior with a particular group or reflect his status. One of the very earliest helmets uncovered belongs to a Sumerian prince (drawing 2) called Mes-kalam-dug. Uncovered in his tomb in Ur, it is made of electrum, a natural alloy of gold and silver. It is beaten out of one sheet of metal and covers the head and ears. It was provided with a padding of thick cloth and so was intended to be worn, not merely symbolic, but its thinness means it would be of little protection in a battle. Similarly shaped helmets (drawing 1), but less ornately decorated and probably more robustly constructed, are shown on representations of Sumerian warriors.

New Kingdom Egyptian pharaohs in battle are portrayed wearing the khepresh or war-crown (drawing 3). The helmet was made of leather coloured blue and was covered with small gold or bronze discs. A sacred cobra was fixed to the brow of the helmet and yellow ribbons were tied to the neck guard. Ordinary New Kingdom Egyptian warriors wore a striped head-dress (drawings 4 and 5), which may have been strengthened by having leather strips fastened to a cloth base.

The Assyrians took the use of armour more seriously and their warriors wore iron helmets (drawings 6 and 7). Generally following a tall conical shape, some had ear pieces attached to them, either as flexible hinged pieces or as part of the integral design. Many were inlaid with bronze, bronze bands sometimes indicating rank. Associated allied troops wore different shaped helmets with different shaped crests. Assyrian rulers, such as the mighty Tiglath-Pileser III, wore a distinctive cap or "polo crown" with a cone on top (drawing 8), derived from Kassite Babylonian court dress.

The Philistines have been identified as one of the Sea-Peoples that battled with the Egyptians. Located in Palestine, they are portrayed as wearing a very distinctive head-dress (drawing 9). Once thought to be made of feathers, the crown of this hat is now thought to be made either of reeds, horsehair, or perhaps stiffened strips of leather. This was held in place by a decorated headband and secured with a chin strap.

Persian warriors were influenced by their own native style and that of the Medes, living to the north of them and for some time the more dominant power. The Medes, in turn, were influenced by the steppe culture of central Asia, such as the Scythians. The soft caps worn mostly by Persian soldiers (drawings 11 and 12) are of Median influence and are the headgear most commonly portrayed on Greek vase paintings. The long ear pieces were often tied under the chin. Bronze or iron helmets were less common (drawing 10) but are shown being worn by Persian cavalry.

HANEY

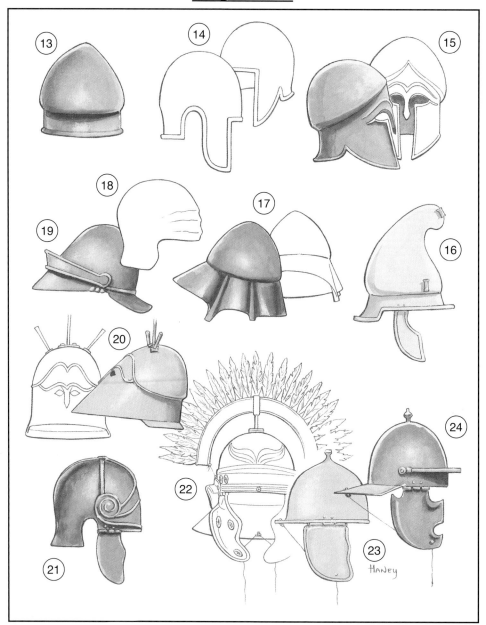

A revolution occurred in ancient helmet design with the Greeks. Along with their adoption of bronze breastplates for the decisive contact warfare favoured by hoplites, so helmets became more defensive and covered more of the face, helping the hoplite to survive in the deadly scrum of phalanx warfare. Earlier, pre-hoplite Greek helmets of the Mycenean period (drawing 13) were simple round bronze caps. By the 8th century BC, this had become more complex. The Corinthian helmet (drawing 15) was an extraordinary development and remains perhaps the most elegant of ancient helmets today.

Hammered out of a single piece of metal, the Corinthian had no separate attached cheek pieces, but these proceeded from the skull and were extended around the back of the head to protect the neck. In front, the extended cheek pieces left just a T-shaped gap for the eyes and mouth with the nose sometimes being protected by a nasal extending from the brow. It was perfectly designed for phalanx warfare in which the hoplite had as much to fear from a friendly spear or sword blow from the back as the spear points in front of him. Its disadvantage was that it severely reduced the hearing of the wearer, but then the hoplite was only concerned with forward attack and so this probably helped cut out any terrifying sounds around him. A less complex form of Greek helmet was the Illyrian (drawing 14).

By the late 5th century BC, more flexible forms of warfare had evolved in Greek society and the Corinthian helmet went out of fashion as warriors required more awareness of the battle situation around them. The Thracian helmet (drawing 16) came into vogue, being a metal version of the Phrygian woollen or cloth caps worn by more Asian warriors. These had separate cheek pieces and plumes could be inserted into holders on the side. Another open style of bronze helmet favoured by Alexander's Macedonian cavalry was the Boeotian helmet (drawing 17). Hannibal's Carthaginian warriors wore bronze helmets of similar Hellenistic influence (drawings 18, 19 and 21).

Republican Roman helmets followed their own pattern of development, but were influenced by two distinctive cultures, Hellenistic Greek and Celtic. The so-called Etrusco-Corinthian helmet (drawing 20) was clearly based on early Greek models but is even more enclosed. A beautiful example found in Melfi in Apulia retains holders for a crest and two feathers. This helmet type has been associated with the triarii in the Roman legion, the older, wealthier veterans of the army who fought in the last line, while the younger hastati and principes are believed to have worn the more popular Montefortino style helmet (drawing 23). Reputedly based on Celtic models, this simple open bronze helmet had attachable cheek pieces and a single plume-holder. This later evolved into the Coolus type, with extended neck guard and cheek guards, worn by most Roman legionaries (drawing 24), being more highly decorated when worn by senior officers such as centurions (drawing 22).

HANEY